SRA

Early Interventions in Reading

Level 1

Placement and Assessment Guide

Columbus, OH

The McGraw-Hill Companies

SRAonline.com

Send all inquiries to:
SRA/McGraw-Hill
8787 Orion Place
Columbus, OH 43240-4027

Printed in the United States of America.

ISBN 0-07-602672-8

3 4 5 6 7 8 9 VHG 09 08 07 06

The McGraw·Hill Companies

Table of Contents

Placing Students

Placement Overview 1

Administering the Screening Test 2

Administering the Placement Test 2

Screening Test Record 3

Screening Test 5

Placement Test Record 7

Placement Test 8

Assessing Mastery

Measurement Overview 11

Fluency Goals 11

Lesson Mastery Sheet 11

Student Assessments 21

Administering Student Assessments 21

Group Summary Record 22

Assessment Record Sheets and Assessments 23

Program Blackline Masters

Mini Vowel Cards Blackline Master 83

Consonant Digraph Cards Blackline Master .83

Time to Shine Reading Certificate Blackline Master

English 84

Spanish 85

Placing Students

Placement Overview

In order to appropriately place students in the ***SRA Early Interventions in Reading*** program, you should administer a reliable and valid screening measure during the first several weeks of the school year. Many schools and classrooms are routinely beginning to give such tests to all students at the beginning of the year. If such tests are not routine in your school, initial teacher observations can be helpful in spotting students who should be screened to determine if they would benefit from ***SRA Early Interventions in Reading.***

One quick way to spot students likely to need this intervention is to watch for students who are struggling to master the letter-sound, blending, and decoding instruction provided during the first several weeks of the school year. Students who consistently struggle with phonemic awareness activities during instruction may also need the extra help provided by the program. Of course, it becomes easier to notice students who are not making adequate progress as each week passes. However, it is important to identify students who need extra help as soon as possible because every day that passes allows students to fall farther and farther behind their peers. Our goal for all students is grade-level reading skills by the end of the year; the farther behind children fall at any point in the year, the more difficult it is for them to achieve that goal.

There are a number of tests currently available that can be used to screen students who need the support provided in ***SRA Early Interventions in Reading.*** These tests are described in more detail in the Program Overview in the **Teacher's Editions.**

Another method for determining placement is the use of the in-program screening tool. In situations where no schoolwide test is given, or if a student moves into your classroom after the school year has started, you may want to administer the Screening Test to help determine whether a student would benefit from the intervention instruction. Results of the screening test have the potential to help you identify students at risk of failing in reading earlier in the school year.

Placing students in the appropriate lessons is an essential part of ensuring student success in ***SRA Early Interventions in Reading.*** Once a student has been identified as potentially benefiting from an early intervention curriculum, through either an outside test of skills or the in-program Screening Test, administer the Placement Test to students. The Placement Test consists of a series of short activities designed to mirror the content of the intervention materials at different points in the curriculum. Based on a student's demonstrated mastery of the skills in each of the Placement Test sections, either administer the next section of the test to the student, place the student in a specific lesson within the curriculum, or move the student out of the intervention group to receive instruction in only the primary reading materials.

Administering the Screening Test

As mentioned in the Placement Overview, you may elect to administer the in-program Screening Test to help you determine whether a student should be placed in the ***SRA Early Interventions in Reading*** program when schoolwide test results are unavailable or if a student moves into your classroom after the school year has started. To administer the Screening Test, make a copy of the Screening Test Record (pages 3–4) for each student who will complete the Screening Test. Provide each student with a copy of the Screening Test (pages 5–6). Administer the Screening Test to each student, following the directions on the Screening Test Record. Mark and record errors as indicated on the record sheet. Stop administration as directed. Place the student in Lesson 1 of ***SRA Early Interventions in Reading,*** Level 1, in the regular classroom reading program only, or administer the Placement Test if additional information is needed to ensure correct lesson placement.

Administering the Placement Test

A Placement Test has been provided to help ensure appropriate student placement in the ***SRA Early Interventions in Reading*** materials. Make a copy of the Placement Test Record (page 7) for each student completing the Placement Test. Provide each student with a copy of the Placement Test (pages 8–10). Administer the Placement Test to each student, following the directions on the Placement Test Record. Have each student start with Section 1 on the Placement Test. Direct the student to read the list of words and then to read the sentence. Mark each error on the Placement Test Record with a slash (/). Stop administration as directed. Identify and record the student's placement information at the top of the Placement Test Record.

Student____________________________ **Date**____________

Screening Test Record

Placement

- ❏ **Teacher's Edition A,** Lesson 1
- ❏ Administer Placement Test
- ❏ No ***SRA Early Interventions in Reading*** Placement

Administration

(Before administering the assessment, make a copy of this record form for each student being tested. Fill out the top of the forms with the students' names and testing date. Make a copy of the Screening Test for the student.)

(Hold up a copy of the Screening Test. Point to Part 1 on the page.)

Part 1: Story Reading

I have a story I want you to read for me today. Read this story as fast as you can without making a mistake.
(Point to the first word of the title, and say, "Begin here." Start the stopwatch.)

As student reads, mark each error with a dark slash (/).

Errors include:

- Omissions
- Insertions
- Mispronunciations not caused by a speech defect (for example, *house* instead of *home* or leaving off inflectional endings *-s, -ed,* and *-ing*)
- Words requiring more than 4 seconds

If a student cannot read a word within 4 seconds, put a slash (/) through the word on the record sheet, tell student to go to the next word, and point to the next word in the sentence.

The Mat

Dad sat on the mat.

Mom sat with Dad.

Nan and Sam sat with Mom and Dad.

The cat sat in Mom's lap.

Time:________

Errors:________

✓ If student makes 1 or no errors in 45 seconds or less, discontinue testing. Place student in regular classroom reading instruction only.

✓ If student makes 2 or more errors, or if he or she requires more than 45 seconds to read the passage, administer Part 2.

Part 2—Activity A: Letter Knowledge

Tell me the names for these letters. *(Point under each letter. If the student does not respond within 2 seconds, move to the next letter. Place a slash (/) through each letter missed.)*

d a m r t

n f c I

✓ If the student makes 2 or more errors, discontinue testing. Place the student in Lesson 1 of ***SRA Early Interventions in Reading,*** Level 1.

✓ If student makes 1 or no errors, continue testing.

Part 2—Activity B: Initial Sound

I will say a word. Tell me the first sound you hear in the word. I will do the first one. *Mmmat.* The first sound in *mmmat* is */mmm/.*

Your turn.

1. ***Fan.* Tell me the first sound you hear in *fffan.***

   Correct_____ Incorrect_____

2. ***Net.* Tell me the first sound you hear in *nnnet.***

   Correct_____ Incorrect_____

3. ***Dish.* Tell me the first sound you hear in *dish.***

   Correct_____ Incorrect_____

4. ***Boat.* Tell me the first sound you hear in *boat.***

   Correct_____ Incorrect_____

5. ***Star.* Tell me the first sound you hear in *ssstar.***

   Correct_____ Incorrect_____

✓ If student makes 1 or more errors, discontinue testing. Place student in Lesson 1 of ***SRA Early Interventions in Reading,*** Level 1.

✓ If student makes no errors, continue screening with Activity C.

Part 2—Activity C: Word Reading

I want you to read these words. *(Point under each word on student's copy. If student does not read a word within 3 seconds, move to the next word. Place a slash (/) through each word missed.)*

High-Frequency Sight Words

is	to
said	yes
the	sat
I	no
me	was

✓ If student makes 2 or more errors, discontinue testing. Place student in Lesson 1 of ***SRA Early Interventions in Reading,*** Level 1.

✓ If student makes 1 or no errors, continue with decodable words.

Decodable Words

Am	At
Sat	rat
Sam	sand

✓ If student makes 4 or more errors, discontinue testing. Place student in Lesson 1 of ***SRA Early Interventions in Reading,*** Level 1

✓ If student makes 1–3 errors, administer Placement Test to determine the appropriate lesson placement.

✓ If student makes no errors, place him or her in regular classroom reading instruction only.

Screening Test

Part 1

The Mat

Dad sat on the mat.

Mom sat with Dad.

Nan and Sam sat
with Mom and Dad.

The cat sat in Mom's lap.

Part 2

d a m r t

n f c I

is	to	Am
said	yes	At
the	sat	Sat
I	no	rat
me	was	Sam
		sand

Student ____________________ Date __________

Placement Test Record

Placement	
Teacher's Edition ______	Lesson ______

Section 1 *Number of Errors* ____	ant sits have is and Tim was Nan and Sam sit in the sand.	**1 or no errors:** Continue to Section 2. **2 or more errors:** Stop administration. Place student in **Teacher's Edition A, Lesson 1.**
Section 2 *Number of Errors* ____	far crab back card crib can't Jan is on a ship with her pet frog.	**1 or no errors:** Continue to Section 3. **2 or more errors:** Stop administration. Place student in **Teacher's Edition A, Lesson 21.**
Section 3 *Number of Errors* ____	smelled mix bucket truck stars I packed a tent for the camping trip.	**1 or no errors:** Continue to Section 4. **2 or more errors:** Stop administration. Place student in **Teacher's Edition B, Lesson 41.**
Section 4 *Number of Errors* ____	finish under yelled dishes pitch cape The bucket was filled with cold water.	**1 or no errors:** Continue to Section 5. **2 or more errors:** Stop administration. Place student in **Teacher's Edition B, Lesson 61.**
Section 5 *Number of Errors* ____	stone perfect stronger refuse sailing The cute baby cubs were playing in the forest.	**1 or no errors:** Continue to Section 6. **2 or more errors:** Stop administration. Place student in **Teacher's Edition C, Lesson 81.**
Section 6 *Number of Errors* ____	flying clerk peanut family concert Father is taking the family to a concert in the park.	**1 or no errors:** Place in Level 2. **2 or more errors:** Stop administration. Place student in **Teacher's Edition C, Lesson 81.**

Placement Test
Sections 1–2

ant sits have is
and Tim was

Nan and Sam sit
in the sand.

---

far crab back
card crib can't

Jan is on a ship
with her pet frog.

Sections 3–4

smelled mix bucket
truck stars

I packed a tent for the camping trip.

---

finish under yelled
dishes pitch cape

The bucket was filled with cold water.

Sections 5-6

stone perfect stronger
refuse sailing

The cute baby cubs were playing in the forest.

---

flying clerk peanut
family concert

Father is taking the family to a concert in the park.

Assessing Mastery

Measurement Overview

Every activity in every lesson of ***SRA Early Interventions in Reading*** should be taught to mastery to ensure maximum student success. Teaching to mastery allows students to build on the skills and knowledge they gain in each lesson. ***SRA Early Interventions in Reading*** provides several tools to help you monitor student progress and assess student mastery of lesson materials. Through a combination of teacher observation and the use of in-program mastery measurement tools, at-risk students will receive the instruction they need to become successful readers.

Fluency Goals

Starting in Lesson 33, a fluency goal is provided for each connected text reading activity. Students begin reading at a pace of 20 words per minute. Monitor students to make sure they are reading smoothly and with expression while working toward the fluency goals that are listed in the **Teacher's Edition** dialogues. By the end of Level 1 of ***SRA Early Interventions in Reading,*** students demonstrate normal fluency levels of 60 words per minute on end-of-first-grade text.

Success meeting fluency goals is initially monitored as a group measurement through individual practice. Beginning in Lesson 92, with the introduction of Partner Reading: Beat the Clock, you will assess fluency levels both for the group and for individual students. Fluency progress is recorded in the Fluency portion of the Lesson Mastery Sheet for group reading and partner reading.

Lesson Mastery Sheet

The Lesson Mastery Sheet (pages 12–20) provides visual reinforcement of student progress and mastery for the ***SRA Early Interventions in Reading*** materials. Because mastery is generally assessed during the independent practice portions of each activity, the Lesson Mastery Sheet provides a graphic representation of lesson progress and skill mastery to ensure and encourage successful completion of lesson materials. Tracking student mastery on the Lesson Mastery Sheet helps ensure that each activity is being taught to mastery before a lesson is completed.

At the end of each activity, tell students whether they have mastered the skill being taught. If they have, you will put a check mark on the Lesson Mastery Sheet. This check indicates that every student in the group demonstrated mastery for the skill independently with no mistakes. If an error occurs during individual practice, provide additional instruction and additional group practice followed by another round of individual turns. Repeat this process until all students are able to perform the skill independently without error. At the end of each lesson, when all skills in the lesson have been mastered, place a sticker in the Mastery column to indicate mastery of the entire lesson.

The Lesson Mastery Sheet appears on the following pages. Make a copy of the Lesson Mastery Sheet for each group you are teaching.

Lesson Mastery Sheet

Teacher ______________________ **Group** ______________________

Students ______________________ ______________________

______________________ ______________________

______________________ ______________________

Lesson \ Activity	1	2	3	4	5	6	7	8	9	10	Fluency		Mastery
1									★	★			
2													
3									★	★			
4													
5													
6								★	★	★			
7										★			
8									★	★			
9													
10										★			

Make one copy for each group of students.

Lesson Mastery Sheet

Lesson	Activity	1	2	3	4	5	6	7	8	9	10	Fluency		Mastery
	11													
	12								★	★	★			
	13										★			
	14									★	★			
	15										★			
	16									★	★			
	17										★			
	18										★			
	19									★	★			
	20									★	★			
	21										★			
	22									★	★			
	23									★	★			
	24										★			
	25									★	★			

Lesson Mastery Sheet

Lesson / Activity	1	2	3	4	5	6	7	8	9	10	Fluency		Mastery
26									★	★			
27									★	★			
28									★	★			
29										★			
30										★			
31													
32									★	★			
33										★	Group Yes / No		
34									★	★	Group Yes / No		
35									★	★	Group Yes / No		
36										★	Group Yes / No		
37										★	Group Yes / No		
38									★	★	Group Yes / No		
39										★	Group Yes / No		
40										★	Group Yes / No		

Lesson Mastery Sheet

Lesson / Activity	1	2	3	4	5	6	7	8	9	10	Fluency		Mastery
41										★	Group Yes / No		
42										★	Group Yes / No		
43										★	Group Yes / No		
44										★	Group Yes / No		
45									★	★	Group Yes / No		
46									★	★	Group Yes / No		
47									★	★	Group Yes / No		
48										★	Group Yes / No		
49									★	★	Group Yes / No		
50									★	★	Group Yes / No		
51									★	★	Group Yes / No		
52									★	★	Group Yes / No		
53								★	★	★	Group Yes / No		
54								★	★	★	Group Yes / No		
55								★	★	★	Group Yes / No		

Lesson Mastery Sheet

Lesson / Activity	1	2	3	4	5	6	7	8	9	10	Fluency	Mastery
56									★	★	Group Yes / No	
57								★	★	★	Group Yes / No	
58										★	Group Yes / No	
59									★	★	Group Yes / No	
60								★	★	★	Group Yes / No	
61											Group Yes / No	
62								★	★	★	Group Yes / No	
63									★	★	Group Yes / No	
64								★	★	★	Group Yes / No	
65									★	★	Group Yes / No	
66								★	★	★	Group Yes / No	
67								★	★	★	Group Yes / No	
68							★	★	★	★	Group Yes / No	
69									★	★	Group Yes / No	
70							★	★	★	★	Group Yes / No	

Lesson Mastery Sheet

Lesson / Activity	1	2	3	4	5	6	7	8	9	10	Fluency		Mastery
71									★	★	Group Yes / No		
72								★	★	★	Group Yes / No		
73								★	★	★	Group Yes / No		
74								★	★	★	Group Yes / No		
75								★	★	★	Group Yes / No		
76								★	★	★	Group Yes / No		
77							★	★	★	★	Group Yes / No		
78								★	★	★	Group Yes / No		
79									★	★	Group Yes / No		
80								★	★	★	Group Yes / No		
81									★	★	Group Yes / No		
82								★	★	★	Group Yes / No		
83									★	★	Group Yes / No		
84								★	★	★	Group Yes / No		
85									★	★	Group Yes / No		

Lesson Mastery Sheet

Lesson / Activity	1	2	3	4	5	6	7	8	9	10	Fluency (Group)	Fluency (Student)	Mastery
86									★	★	Group Yes / No		
87							★	★	★	★	Group Yes / No		
88								★	★	★	Group Yes / No		
89								★	★	★	Group Yes / No		
90										★	Group Yes / No		
91									★	★	Group Yes / No		
92								★	★	★	Group Yes / No	Student Yes / No	
93								★	★	★	Group Yes / No	Student Yes / No	
94							★	★	★	★	Group Yes / No		
95						★	★	★	★	★	Group Yes / No		
96						★	★	★	★	★	Group Yes / No	Student Yes / No	
97								★	★	★	Group Yes / No	Student Yes / No	
98								★	★	★	Group Yes / No	Student Yes / No	
99							★	★	★	★	Group Yes / No		
100								★	★	★	Group Yes / No	Student Yes / No	

Lesson Mastery Sheet

Lesson / Activity	1	2	3	4	5	6	7	8	9	10	Fluency: Group	Fluency: Student	Mastery
101							★	★	★	★	Yes / No	Yes / No	
102									★	★	Yes / No	Yes / No	
103									★	★	Yes / No	Yes / No	
104							★	★	★	★	Yes / No	Yes / No	
105							★	★	★	★	Yes / No		
106								★	★	★	Yes / No	Yes / No	
107								★	★	★	Yes / No	Yes / No	
108						★	★	★	★	★	Yes / No	Yes / No	
109								★	★	★	Yes / No	Yes / No	
110								★	★	★	Yes / No	Yes / No	
111							★	★	★	★	Yes / No	Yes / No	
112								★	★	★	Yes / No	Yes / No	
113								★	★	★	Yes / No		
114							★	★	★	★	Yes / No	Yes / No	
115								★	★	★	Yes / No		

Lesson Mastery Sheet

Lesson / Activity	1	2	3	4	5	6	7	8	9	10	Fluency: Group	Fluency: Student	Mastery
116								★	★	★	Group Yes / No	Student Yes / No	
117								★	★	★	Group Yes / No		
118								★	★	★	Group Yes / No		
119							★	★	★	★	Group Yes / No	Student Yes / No	
120							★	★	★	★	Group Yes / No	Student Yes / No	

Student Assessments

A series of student assessments is provided to assess student mastery of the skills presented in each of the **Teacher's Editions.** Students are assessed for mastery and generalization of letter-sound correspondences, word reading, and connected text. An assessment is administered every sixth or eighth lesson. For the first six assessments, each assessment is timed for one minute. Starting in **Teacher's Edition B,** students also read a passage they have previously read. You will time each student reading for one minute. Fluency is calculated as words correct per minute (wcpm), with the fluency goal for the assessments listed in the teacher's materials.

These in-program assessments represent a powerful tool for both monitoring student progress and evaluating your presentation of lesson content. Student performance on the assessments allows you to evaluate if students are learning what you are teaching, indicates if your lesson-presentation pacing is appropriate, and helps you determine when reteaching is necessary and when to move on without reteaching. Administering the student assessments is a valuable way to ensure that students truly are mastering lesson content and building the foundation for skills introduced in subsequent lessons.

Administering Student Assessments

To administer the student assessments, make a copy of the appropriate Assessment Record for each student in the group. Provide each student with a copy of the appropriate student assessment. You will also need a copy of the Group Summary Record (page 22) for each group during each student assessment. Administer the assessment to each student, following the directions on the Assessment Record. Mark and record errors as indicated on the record sheet. Fill out the information at the top of the Group Summary Record, and then tally and record each student's results on the Group Summary Record. In the last column of the Group Summary Record, list any letter-sounds or words that students missed on the assessment. Before starting the next lesson, write on the marker board any items requiring additional practice. Using the model-lead-test strategy, review the letter-sounds and words with students.

Group Summary Record

Student Assessments

Teacher ______________________ ______________________

Group ______________________ ______________________

Assessment ______________________ **Lessons** ______________________

Name	Date	Letter-Sound Errors	Word Structure Errors	Connected Text Errors	Fluency Passage (wcpm)	Items Requiring Additional Practice

Make one copy for each group of students for each Assessment.

Student ______________________________ **Date** ______________

Assessment 1 – Record Sheet
Lessons 1–6

Goals: 1 minute for total assessment. 100% accuracy for each section.

Administration

(Administer to individual students. Check each box when the student achieves mastery.)

(Before administering the assessment, make a copy of this assessment form for each student being tested. Fill out the top of the forms with the students' names and testing date. Make a copy of student's Assessment 1.)

(Hold up a copy of student's Assessment 1. Point to Part 1 on the page.)

We are going to find out how well you can say letter-sounds. When I touch under a letter, say its sound. Get ready.
(Touch under the first letter on the student's page.)

m❐ t❐ a❐

Say the sound.
(Pause no more than 2 seconds to allow the student to respond. If the student responds correctly, check the box beside the letter on your copy of the assessment. Repeat the procedure with the next two letters.)

(Point to Part 2 on the student's page.)
We are going to find out how well you can sound out words. When I touch under a letter, say its sound. Keep saying its sound until I touch under the next letter. Get ready.

(Touch under the first word in Part 2 on the student's page.)

mat❐ am❐

(Touch under each letter, moving your finger along the arrow and stopping at the final dot. If the student responds correctly, check the box beside the word on your copy of the assessment. Repeat the procedure with the next word.)

(Point to Part 3 on the student's page.)
Now we will find out how well you can read words in a sentence. First, write your name on the line, and read your name. *(Pause.)*

When I tap under a tricky word, you will read it. When I slide my finger under a word with dots, you will sound out the word. When I tap under your name, you will read it. Then you will read the entire sentence the fast way.
(Tap under the tricky word; move your finger slowly under the word to be decoded; tap under the student's name. If the student responds correctly, check the box beside the sentence on your copy of the assessment.)

I am ____________________.❐

Remediation

(Before starting Lesson 7, review any letter-sounds or words students had trouble with on Assessment 1. Write on the marker board the items students missed. Using the model-lead-test strategy, review the letter-sounds and words with students.)

Assessment 1

Lessons 1–6

Part 1

m t a

Part 2

mat am

Part 3

I am ________.

Student____________________________ Date__________

Assessment 2–Record Sheet

Lessons 7–12

Goals: 1 minute for total assessment. 100% accuracy for each section.

Administration

(Administer to individual students. Check each box when the student achieves mastery.)

(Before administering the assessment, make a copy of this assessment form for each student being tested. Fill out the top of the forms with the students' names and testing date. Make a copy of student's Assessment 2.)

(Hold up a copy of student's Assessment 2. Point to Part 1 on the page.)

We are going to find out how well you can say letter-sounds. When I touch under a letter, say its sound. Get ready.
(Touch under the first letter on the student's page.)

d☐ s☐ r☐

Say the sound.
(Pause no more than 2 seconds to allow the student to respond. If the student responds correctly, check the box beside the letter on your copy of the assessment. Repeat the procedure with the next two letters.)

(Point to Part 2 on the student's page.)
We are going to find out how well you can sound out words. When I touch under a letter, say its sound. Keep saying its sound until I touch under the next letter. Get ready.

(Touch under the first word in Part 2 on the student's page.)

sad☐ ram☐

(Touch under each letter, moving your finger along the arrow and stopping at the final dot.)

Now read the word the fast way.
(If the student responds correctly, check the box beside the word on your copy of the assessment. Repeat the procedure with the next word.)

(Point to Part 3 on the student's page.)
Now we will find out how well you can read words in a sentence. *(Pause.)*

When I tap under a tricky word, you will read it. When I slide my finger under a word with dots, you will sound out the word and read it. Then you will read the entire sentence the fast way.
(Tap under each tricky word; move your finger slowly under words to be decoded. If the student responds correctly, check the box beside the sentence on your copy of the assessment.)

I am a rat on a mat.☐

Remediation

(Before starting Lesson 13, review any letter-sounds or words students had trouble with on Assessment 2. Write on the marker board the items students missed. Using the model-lead-test strategy, review the letter-sounds and words with students.)

Assessment 2
Lessons 7–12

Part 1

d s r

Part 2

sad ram

Part 3

I am a rat on a mat.

Student ______________________________ **Date** ______________

Assessment 3 – Record Sheet

Lessons 13–20

Goals: 1 minute for total assessment.
100% accuracy for each section.

Administration

(Administer to individual students. Check each box when the student achieves mastery.)

(Before administering the assessment, make a copy of this assessment form for each student being tested. Fill out the top of the forms with the students' names and testing date. Make a copy of student's Assessment 3.)

(Hold up a copy of student's Assessment 3. This time, provide the student a copy of the assessment as well. Point to Part 1 on the student's page.)

We are going to find out how well you can say letter-sounds. When I touch under a letter, say its sound. Get ready.
(Touch under the first letter on the student's page.)

c❐ n❐ f❐ i❐

Say the sound.
(Pause no more than 2 seconds to allow the student to respond. If the student responds correctly, check the box beside the letter on your copy of the assessment. Repeat the procedure with the remaining sounds.)

(Point to Part 2 on the student's page.)
We are going to find out how well you can sound out words. When I touch under a letter, say its sound. Keep saying its sound until I touch under the next letter. Then read the word the fast way. Get ready.

(Touch under the first word in Part 2 on the student's page.)

fin❐ sand❐

Sound it out.
(Slide your finger under the letters as student sounds out the first word.)

Now read the word the fast way.
(If the student responds correctly, check the box beside the word on your copy of the assessment. Repeat the procedure with the next word.)

(Point to Part 3 on the student's page.)
Now we will find out how well you can read words in a sentence. *(Pause.)*

When I tap under a word, you will read it. When I slide my finger under a word, you will sound out the word and then read it fast. Then you will read the entire sentence the fast way.
(Tap under each tricky word; move your finger slowly under words to be decoded. If the student responds correctly, check the box beside the sentence on your copy of the assessment.)

The ant is in the sand.❐

Remediation

(Before starting Lesson 21, review any letter-sounds or words students had trouble with on Assessment 3. Write on the marker board the items students missed. Using the model-lead-test strategy, review the letter-sounds and words with students.)

Assessment 3

Lessons 13–20

Part 1

c n f i

Part 2

fin sand

Part 3

The ant is in the sand.

Student ______________________ Date __________

Assessment 4—Record Sheet
Lessons 21–26

Goals: 1 minute for total assessment. 100% accuracy for each section.

Administration

(Administer to individual students. Check each box when the student achieves mastery.)

(Before administering the assessment, make a copy of this assessment form for each student being tested. Fill out the top of the forms with the students' names and testing date. Make a copy of student's Assessment 4.)

(Provide the student a copy of Assessment 4. Point to Part 1 on the student's page.)

We are going to find out how well you can say letter-sounds. When you touch under a letter, say its sound. Get ready.
(Have student touch under p *on his or her copy, and say, "Say the sound.")*

p☐ h☐

Say the sound.
(Pause no more than 2 seconds to allow the student to respond. If the student responds correctly, check the box beside the letter on your copy of the assessment. Repeat the procedure with h.*)*

(Point to Part 2 on the student's page.)
We are going to find out how well you can sound out words on your own. Touch under each letter when I tap, and say the sound. Keep saying the sound until I tap again. Hum the word, and then read it the fast way. Get ready.

(Touch under the first word in Part 2 on the student's page.)

fact☐ cast☐ pat☐

Sound it out.
(Slide your finger under the letters as the student sounds out the first word.)

Now read the word the fast way.
(If the student responds correctly, check the box beside the word on your copy of the assessment. Repeat the procedure with the remaining words.)

(Point to Part 3 on the student's page.)
Now we will find out how well you can read words in a sentence. *(Pause.)*

Sound out each word, and then read it fast. Then read the entire sentence the fast way.
(Have student point under each letter, say the sound, and then read the word fast. Then have student read the sentence the fast way. The student will read tricky words without sounding out. If the student responds correctly, check the box beside the sentence on your copy of the assessment.)

It is a fast raft.☐

Remediation

(Before starting Lesson 27, review any letter-sounds or words students had trouble with on Assessment 4. Write on the marker board the items students missed. Using the model-lead-test strategy, review the letter-sounds and words with students.)

Assessment 4
Lessons 21–26

Part 1

p h

Part 2

fact cast pat

Part 3

It is a fast raft.

Student________________________________ Date______________

Assessment 5—Record Sheet

Lessons 27–32

Goals: 1 minute for total assessment. 100% accuracy for each section.

Administration

(Administer to individual students. Check each box when the student achieves mastery.)

(Before administering the assessment, make a copy of this assessment form for each student being tested. Fill out the top of the forms with the students' names and testing date. Make a copy of student's Assessment 5.)

(Provide the student a copy of Assessment 5. Point to Part 1 on the student's page.)

We are going to find out how well you can say letter-sounds. When you touch under a letter-sound, say its sound. Get ready. *(Have student touch under the first letter-sound on his or her copy, and say, "Say the sound.")*

sh❒ g❒ o❒

Say the sound.
(Pause no more than 2 seconds to allow the student to respond. If the student responds correctly, check the box beside the letter-sound on your copy of the test. Repeat the procedure with the remaining letter-sounds.)

(Point to Part 2 on the student's page.) **We are going to find out how well you can sound out words on your own. Touch under each letter when I tap, and say the sound. Keep saying the sound until I tap again. Hum the word, and then read it the fast way. Get ready.**

(Touch under the first word in Part 2 on the student's page.)

gift❒ soft❒ dish❒

Sound it out.
(Slide your finger under the letters as student sounds out the first word.)

Now read the word the fast way.
(If the student responds correctly, check the box beside the word on your copy of the assessment. Repeat the procedure with the remaining words.)

(Point to Part 3 on the student's page.) **Now we will find out how well you can read words in a sentence.** *(Pause.)*

Sound out each word, and then read it fast. Then read the entire sentence the fast way.
(Have student point under each letter, say the sound, and then read the word fast. Then have student read the sentence the fast way. The student will read tricky words without sounding out. If the student responds correctly, check the box beside the sentence on your copy of the assessment.)

The cat had a nap on the mat.❒

Remediation

(Before starting Lesson 33, review any letter-sounds or words students had trouble with on Assessment 5. Write on the marker board the items students missed. Using the model-lead-test strategy, review the letter-sounds and words with students.)

Assessment 5

Lessons 27–32

Part 1

sh g o

Part 2

gift soft dish

Part 3

The cat had a nap on the mat.

Student ______________________ Date ________

Assessment 6— Record Sheet
Lessons 33–40

Goals: 1 minute for total assessment. 100% accuracy for each section.

Administration

(Administer to individual students. Check each box when the student achieves mastery.)

(Before administering the assessment, make a copy of this assessment form for each student being tested. Fill out the top of the forms with the students' names and testing date. Make a copy of student's Assessment 6.)

(Provide the student a copy of Assessment 6. Point to Part 1 on the student's page.)

We are going to find out how well you can say letter-sounds. When you touch under a letter-sound, say its sound. Get ready. *(Have students touch under the first letter-sound on their copy, and say, "Say the sound.")*

x❐ ar❐ b❐ ck❐

Say the sound.
(Pause no more than 2 seconds to allow the student to respond. If the student responds correctly, check the box beside the letter-sound on your copy of the test. Repeat the procedure with the remaining letter-sounds.)

(Point to Part 2 on the student's page.) **We are going to find out how well you can sound out words on your own. Touch under each letter-sound when I tap, and say the sound. Keep saying the sound until I tap again. Hum the word, and then read it the fast way. Get ready.**

(Touch under the first word in Part 2 on the student's page.)

star❐ crab❐ back❐

Sound it out.
(Slide your finger under the letters as student sounds out the first word.)

Now read the word the fast way.
(If the student responds correctly, check the box beside the word on your copy of the assessment. Repeat the procedure with the remaining words.)

(Point to Part 3 on the student's page.) **Now we will find out how well you read words in a sentence.** *(Pause.)*

You are going to read a sentence fast the first time. You will read the words fast the first time without saying the sounds aloud. You will slide your finger under each word and then read the word. Get ready to read. *(Do not tap during sentence reading. Have your student move his or her finger slowly under words to be decoded. If the student responds correctly and meets the fluency goal, check the box beside the sentence on your copy of the assessment. Fluency Goal: 3 seconds per word = 21 seconds.)*

The crab hits Dan on the hand.❐

Remediation

(Before starting Lesson 41, review any letter-sounds or words students had trouble with on Assessment 6. Write on the marker board the items students missed. Using the model-lead-test strategy, review the letter-sounds and words with students.)

Assessment 6

Lessons 33–40

Part 1

x ar b ck

Part 2

star crab back

Part 3

The crab hits Dan on the hand.

Student ______________________ Date ____________

Assessment 7 – Record Sheet

Lessons 41–46

Goals: 2 minutes for total assessment. 100% accuracy for Parts 1–3. 23 words correct per minute for Part 4.

Administration

(Administer to individual students. Check each box when the student achieves mastery.)

(Before administering the assessment, make a copy of this assessment form for each student being tested. Fill out the top of the forms with the students' names and testing date. Make a copy of student's Assessment 7.)

(Provide the student a copy of Assessment 7. Point to Part 1 on the student's page.)

We are going to find out how well you can say letter-sounds. When you touch under a letter-sound, say its sound. Get ready.
(Have student touch under the first letter-sound on his or her copy, and say, "Say the sound.")

th (as in this)☐ l☐ e☐

Say the sound.
(Allow no more than 2 seconds for the student to respond. If the student responds correctly, check the box beside the letter-sound on your copy of the test. Repeat the procedure with the remaining letter-sounds.)

(Point to Part 2 on the student's page.)
We are going to find out how well you can sound out words. You will sound out each word part, read each part fast, and then read the whole word the fast way. Get ready.

(Touch under the first word in Part 2 on the student's page.)

rabbit☐ picnic☐ clock☐

Sound out each part, read each part fast, and then read the whole word.
(Have student sound out each part, read each part, and then read the whole word. If the student responds correctly, check the box beside the word on your copy of the assessment. Repeat the procedure with the remaining words.)

(Point to Part 3 on the student's page.)
Now we will find out how well you can read words in a sentence. *(Pause.)*

Read the sentence. If you know the word, say it. If you do not know the word, sound it out to yourself, and say it fast.
(If the student responds correctly, check the box beside the sentence on your copy of the assessment. Fluency Goal: 3 seconds per word = 27 seconds.)

"Yes," said Fox, "but it did not trap you!"☐

Student ______________________________ **Date** ______________

Words Correct Per Minute ________

Fluency

1. Have student read the fluency passage.
2. Time student for one minute.
3. Determine and record the number of words student read correctly in one minute.
4. Fluency Goal = 23 words correct per minute

(Point to Part 4 on the student's page.)
I have a story I want you to read for me today. Read this story as fast as you can without making a mistake.

(Point to the first word of the story, and say, "Begin here." Start the stopwatch.)
As student reads, mark each error with a dark slash (/). At the end of one minute, place a double slash after the last word read in the passage (//).

Errors include:

- Omissions
- Insertions
- Mispronunciations not caused by a speech defect (for example, *house* instead of *home* or leaving off inflectional endings *-s, -ed,* and *-ing*)
- Words requiring more than 4 seconds

If a student cannot read a word within 4 seconds, tell student to go to the next word, put a slash (/) through the word on the record sheet, and point to the next word in the sentence.

After student reads the passage, praise his or her effort reading the passage. Do not offer praise for performance.

Determining number of words read correctly in one minute:

- Count the total number of words read.
- Subtract the number of errors (slashes).
- Write the words read correctly in one minute in the space provided.
- Fluency Goal = 23 words correct per minute

Remediation

(Before starting Lesson 47, review any letter-sounds or words students had trouble with on Assessment 7. Write on the marker board the items students missed. Using the model-lead-test strategy, review the letter-sounds and words with students.)

Rabbit and Fox sat on a big box. 8

"You have a big box," said Rabbit. 15

"Yes," said Fox. "It is a trap." 22

"Can it trap a frog?" said Rabbit. 29

"Yes," said Fox. "It can trap a frog." 37

"Can it trap a cat?" said Rabbit. 44

"Yes," said Fox. "It can trap a cat." 52

Assessment 7

Lessons 41–46

Part 1

th l e

Part 2

rabbit picnic clock

Part 3

“Yes,” said Fox, “but it did not trap you!”

Part 4

Rabbit and Fox sat on a big box.

"You have a big box," said Rabbit.

"Yes," said Fox. "It is a trap."

"Can it trap a frog?" said Rabbit.

"Yes," said Fox. "It can trap a frog."

"Can it trap a cat?" said Rabbit.

"Yes," said Fox. "It can trap a cat."

Student ______________________ Date ____________

Assessment 8–Record Sheet

Lessons 47–52

Goals: 2 minutes for total assessment. 100% accuracy for Parts 1–3. 26 words correct per minute for Part 4.

Administration

(Administer to individual students. Check each box when the student achieves mastery.)

(Before administering the assessment, make a copy of this assessment form for each student being tested. Fill out the top of the forms with the students' names and testing date. Make a copy of student's Assessment 8.)

(Provide the student a copy of Assessment 8. Point to Part 1 on the student's page.)

We are going to find out how well you can say letter-sounds. When you touch under a letter-sound, say its sound. Get ready.
(Have student touch under the first letter-sound on his or her copy, and say, "Say the sound.")

er❒ ch❒ w❒

Say the sound.
(Allow no more than 2 seconds for the student to respond. If the student responds correctly, check the box beside the letter-sound on your copy of the test. Repeat the procedure with the remaining letter-sounds.)

(Point to Part 2 on the student's page.)
We are going to find out how well you can sound out words. You will sound out each word part, read each part fast, and then read the whole word the fast way. Get ready.

(Touch under the first word in Part 2 on the student's page.)

habits❒ wagon❒ speck❒

Sound out each part, read each part fast, and then read the whole word.
(Have student sound out each part, read each part, and then read the whole word. If the student responds correctly, check the box beside the word on your copy of the assessment. Repeat the procedure with the remaining words.)

(Point to Part 3 on the student's page.)
Now we will find out how well you can read words in a sentence. *(Pause.)*

Read each sentence. If you know the word, say it. If you do not know the word, sound it out to yourself, and say it fast.
(If the student responds correctly, check the box beside the sentence on your copy of the assessment. Fluency Goal: 3 seconds per word = 21 seconds for both sentences.)

Gramps grabs at Sinbad.❒

Sinbad acts fast!❒

Student____ **Date**_______________

Words Correct Per Minute ________

Fluency

1. Have student read the fluency passage.
2. Time student for one minute.
3. Determine and record the number of words student read correctly in one minute.
4. Fluency Goal = 26 words correct per minute

(Point to Part 4 on the student's page.)
I have a story I want you to read for me today. Read this story as fast as you can without making a mistake.

(Point to the first word of the story, and say, "Begin here." Start the stopwatch.)
As student reads, mark each error with a dark slash (/). At the end of one minute, place a double slash after the last word read in the passage (//).

Errors include:

- Omissions
- Insertions
- Mispronunciations not caused by a speech defect (for example, *house* instead of *home* or leaving off inflectional endings *-s, -ed,* and *-ing*)
- Words requiring more than 4 seconds

If a student cannot read a word within 4 seconds, tell student to go to the next word, put a slash (/) through the word on the record sheet, and point to the next word in the sentence.

After student reads the passage, praise his or her effort reading the passage. Do not offer praise for performance.

Determining number of words read correctly in one minute:

- Count the total number of words read.
- Subtract the number of errors (slashes).
- Write the words read correctly in one minute in the space provided.
- Fluency Goal = 26 words correct per minute

Remediation

(Before starting Lesson 53, review any letter-sounds or words students had trouble with on Assessment 8. Write on the marker board the items students missed. Using the model-lead-test strategy, review the letter-sounds and words with students.)

"Mom, are stars far away?" 5

"Yes, Max," said Mom. 9

"Stars are far, far away." 14

"Mom, can I have a star?" 20

"Hmm . . . a star . . . ," said Mom. 25

"You sit here, Max," said Mom. 31

"You can have a star here." 37

Max said, "Stars are far away. 43

I can't have a star here." 49

"Here, Max," said Mom. 53

"Here is a star for you." 59

"I have a star!" said Max. 65

"Mom, you are smart!" 69

Assessment 8

Lessons 47–52

Part 1

er ch w

Part 2

habits wagon speck

Part 3

Gramps grabs at Sinbad.

Sinbad acts fast!

Part 4

"Mom, are stars far away?"

"Yes, Max," said Mom.

"Stars are far, far away."

"Mom, can I have a star?"

"Hmm . . . a star . . . ," said Mom.

"You sit here, Max," said Mom.

"You can have a star here."

Max said, "Stars are far away.

I can't have a star here."

"Here, Max," said Mom.

"Here is a star for you."

"I have a star!" said Max.

"Mom, you are smart!"

Student______________________________ **Date**______________

Assessment 9– Record Sheet

Lessons 53–60

Goals: 2 minutes for total assessment. 100% accuracy for Parts 1–3. 30 words correct per minute for Part 4.

Administration

(Administer to individual students. Check each box when the student achieves mastery.)

(Before administering the assessment, make a copy of this assessment form for each student being tested. Fill out the top of the forms with the students' names and testing date. Make a copy of student's Assessment 9.)

(Provide the student a copy of Assessment 9. Point to Part 1 on the student's page.)

We are going to find out how well you can say letter-sounds. When you touch under a letter-sound, say its sound. Get ready.
(Have students touch under the first letter-sound on their copy, and say, "Say the sound.")

ed (pronounced /ed/, /d/, and /t/)☐
ing☐

u☐ th (voiced and unvoiced)☐

Say the sound.
(Allow no more than 2 seconds for the student to respond. For ed *and* th, *make sure students say each sound for the letter-sounds. If the student responds correctly, check the box beside the letter-sound on your copy of the test. Repeat the procedure with the remaining sounds.)*

(Point to Part 2 on the student's page.)
We are going to find out how well you can sound out words. You will sound out each word part, read each part fast, and then read the whole word the fast way. Get ready.
(Touch under the first word in Part 2 on the student's page.)

pres ent☐ camp ing☐ smell ed☐

Sound out each part, read each part fast, and then read the whole word.
(Have student sound out each part, read each part, and then read the whole word. If the student responds correctly, check the box beside the word on your copy of the assessment. Repeat the procedure with the remaining words.)

(Point to Part 3 on the student's page.)
Now we will find out how well you read words in a sentence. *(Pause.)*

Read the sentence. If you know the word, say it. If you do not know the word, sound it out to yourself, and say it fast.
(If the student responds correctly, check the box beside the sentence on your copy of the assessment. Fluency Goal: 2 seconds per word = 20 seconds.)

I camped and tramped, but the fox had a picnic.☐

Student ______________________________ Date ______________

Words Correct Per Minute ______

Fluency

1. Have student read the fluency passage.
2. Time student for one minute.
3. Determine and record the number of words student read correctly in one minute.
4. Fluency Goal = 30 words correct per minute

(Point to Part 4 on the student's page.)
I have a story I want you to read for me today. Read this story as fast as you can without making a mistake.

(Point to the first word of the story, and say, "Begin here." Start the stopwatch.)
As student reads, mark each error with a dark slash (/). At the end of one minute, place a double slash after the last word read in the passage (//).

Errors include:

- Omissions
- Insertions
- Mispronunciations not caused by a speech defect (for example, *house* instead of *home* or leaving off inflectional endings *-s, -ed,* and *-ing*)
- Words requiring more than 4 seconds

If a student cannot read a word within 4 seconds, tell him or her to go to the next word, put a slash (/) through the word on the record sheet, and point to the next word in the sentence.

After student reads the passage, praise his or her effort reading the passage. Do not offer praise for performance.

Determining number of words read correctly in one minute:

- Count the total number of words read.
- Subtract the number of errors (slashes).
- Write the words read correctly in one minute in the space provided.
- Fluency Goal = 30 words correct per minute

Remediation

(Before starting Lesson 61, review any letter-sounds or words students had trouble with on Assessment 9. Write on the marker board the items students missed. Using the model-lead-test strategy, review the letter-sounds and words with students.)

"What is in the bag?" 5

"A bug." 7

"Is it big?" 10

"The bag is big." 14

"No! The bug! Is the bug big?" 21

"In the bag?" 24

"Yes. Is the bug in the bag big?" 32

"It is a big bug bag." 38

"No! Is a big bug in the bag?" 46

"A big bag has the bug." 52

"But the bug! Is the bug big?" 59

"Big bugs bump in bags." 64

"I am not big!" 68

Assessment 9

Lessons 53–60

Part 1

ed ing u th

Part 2

present camping smelled

Part 3

I camped and tramped, but the fox had a picnic.

Part 4

"What is in the bag?"

"A bug."

"Is it big?"

"The bag is big."

"No! The bug! Is the bug big?"

"In the bag?"

"Yes. Is the bug in the bag big?"

"It is a big bug bag."

"No! Is a big bug in the bag?"

"A big bag has the bug."

"But the bug! Is the bug big?"

"Big bugs bump in bags."

"I am not big!"

Student ______________________________ Date ______________

Assessment 10—Record Sheet

Lessons 61–66

Goals: 2 minutes for total assessment.
100% accuracy for Parts 1–3.
33 words correct per minute for Part 4.

Administration

(Administer to individual students. Check each box when the student achieves mastery.)

(Before administering the assessment, make a copy of this assessment form for each student being tested. Fill out the top of the forms with the students' names and testing date. Make a copy of student's Assessment 10.)

(Provide the student a copy of Assessment 10. Point to Part 1 on the student's page.)

We are going to find out how well you can say letter-sounds. When you touch under a letter-sound, say its sound. Get ready.
(Have students touch under the first letter-sound on their copy, and say, "Say the sound.")

z☐ ir☐ y☐ wh☐ ur☐

Say the sound.
(Allow no more than 2 seconds for the student to respond. If the student responds correctly, check the box beside the letter or group on your copy of the test. Repeat the procedure with the remaining sounds.)

(Point to Part 2 on the student's page.)
We are going to find out how well you can read words. First you will read the underlined part. Then you will read the whole word. Get ready.

(Touch under the first word in Part 2 on the student's page.)

started☐ pulling☐ thunder☐

Read the underlined part, and then read the whole word.
(If the student responds correctly, check the box beside the word on your copy of the assessment. Repeat the procedure with the remaining words.)

(Point to Part 3 on the student's page.)
Now we will find out how well you read words in a sentence. *(Pause.)*

Read the sentence. If you know the word, say it. If you do not know the word, sound it out to yourself and say it fast.
(If the student responds correctly, check the box beside the sentence on your copy of the assessment. Fluency Goal: 2 seconds per word = 22 seconds.)

And Zack the One-Man Band
got back on his bus.☐

Student ______________________________ **Date** ______________

Words Correct Per Minute ______

Fluency

1. Have student read the fluency passage.
2. Time student for one minute.
3. Determine and record the number of words student read correctly in one minute.
4. Fluency Goal = 33 words correct per minute

(Point to Part 4 on the student's page.)
I have a story I want you to read for me today. Read this story as fast as you can without making a mistake.

(Point to the first word of the story, and say, "Begin here." Start the stopwatch.)
As student reads, mark each error with a dark slash (/). At the end of one minute, place a double slash after the last word read in the passage (//).

Errors include:

- Omissions
- Insertions
- Mispronunciations not caused by a speech defect (for example, *house* instead of *home* or leaving off inflectional endings *-s, -ed,* and *-ing*)
- Words requiring more than 4 seconds

If a student cannot read a word within 4 seconds, tell student to go to the next word, put a slash (/) through the word on the record sheet, and point to the next word in the sentence.

After student reads the passage, praise his or her effort reading the passage. Do not offer praise for performance.

Determining number of words read correctly in one minute:

- Count the total number of words read.
- Subtract the number of errors (slashes).
- Write the words read correctly in one minute in the space provided.
- Fluency Goal = 33 words correct per minute

Remediation

(Before starting Lesson 67, review any letter-sounds or words students had trouble with on Assessment 10. Write on the marker board the items students missed. Using the model-lead-test strategy, review the letter-sounds and words with students.)

"It is hot," said five pigs. "It is too hot!"	10
The pigs hopped into the pond. Five pigs are in the pond.	22
"It is hot," said four dogs. "It is too hot!"	32
The dogs hopped into the pond. Five pigs and four dogs are in the pond.	47
"It is hot," said three cats. "It is too hot!"	57
The cats hopped into the pond. Five pigs, four dogs, and three cats are in the pond.	74

Assessment 10
Lessons 61–66

Part 1

z ir y wh ur

Part 2

started pulling thunder

Part 3

And Zack the One-Man Band got back on his bus.

Part 4

"It is hot," said five pigs. "It is too hot!"

The pigs hopped into the pond. Five pigs are in the pond.

"It is hot," said four dogs. "It is too hot!"

The dogs hopped into the pond. Five pigs and four dogs are in the pond.

"It is hot," said three cats. "It is too hot!"

The cats hopped into the pond. Five pigs, four dogs, and three cats are in the pond.

Student ______________________________ Date ______________

Assessment 11 – Record Sheet

Lessons 67–72

Goals: 2 minutes for total assessment. 100% accuracy for Parts 1–3. 36 words correct per minute for Part 4.

Administration

(Administer to individual students. Check each box when the student achieves mastery.)

(Before administering the assessment, make a copy of this assessment form for each student being tested. Fill out the top of the forms with the students' names and testing date. Make a copy of student's Assessment 11.)

(Provide the student a copy of Assessment 11. Point to Part 1 on the student's page.)

We are going to find out how well you can say letter-sounds. When you touch under a letter-sound, say its sound. Get ready.
(Have students touch under the first letter-sound on their copy, and say, "Say the sound.")

or❐ al❐ ea (head)❐ all❐

Say the sound.
(Allow no more than 2 seconds for the student to respond. If the student responds correctly, check the box beside the letter-sound on your copy of the test. Repeat the procedure with the remaining sounds.)

(Point to Part 2 on the student's page.)
We are going to find out how well you can read words. First you will read the underlined part. Then you will read the whole word. Get ready.

(Touch under the first word in Part 2 on the student's page.)

instead❐ forget❐ wonderful❐

Read the underlined part, and then read the whole word.
(If the student responds correctly, check the box beside the word on your copy of the assessment. Repeat the procedure with the remaining words.)

(Point to Part 3 on the student's page.)
Now we will find out how well you read words in a sentence. *(Pause.)*

Read the sentence. If you know the word, say it. If you do not know the word, sound it out to yourself and say it fast.
(If the student responds correctly, check the box beside the sentence on your copy of the assessment. Fluency Goal: 2 seconds per word = 12 seconds.)

Deb can't paddle in the pond.❐

Student____ **Date**______________

Words Correct Per Minute _______

Fluency

1. Have student read the fluency passage.
2. Time student for one minute.
3. Determine and record the number of words student read correctly in one minute.
4. Fluency Goal = 36 words correct per minute

(Point to Part 4 on the student's page.)
I have a story I want you to read for me today. Read this story as fast as you can without making a mistake.

(Point to the first word of the story, and say, "Begin here." Start the stopwatch.)
As student reads, mark each error with a dark slash (/). At the end of one minute, place a double slash after the last word read in the passage (//).

Errors include:

- Omissions
- Insertions
- Mispronunciations not caused by a speech defect (for example, *house* instead of *home* or leaving off inflectional endings *-s, -ed,* and *-ing*)
- Words requiring more than 4 seconds

If a student cannot read a word within 4 seconds, tell student to go to the next word, put a slash (/) through the word on the record sheet, and point to the next word in the sentence.

After student reads the passage, praise his or her effort reading the passage. Do not offer praise for performance.

Determining number of words read correctly in one minute:

- Count the total number of words read.
- Subtract the number of errors (slashes).
- Write the words read correctly in one minute in the space provided.
- Fluency Goal = 36 words correct per minute

Remediation

(Before starting Lesson 73, review any letter-sounds or words students had trouble with on Assessment 11. Write on the marker board the items students missed. Using the model-lead-test strategy, review the letter-sounds and words with students.)

Step up! Step up! Tess has a stand! Tess can help! 11

Tess helps all the animals. No problem is too big. No problem is too small. 26

T. Rex wants a snack. "No problem!" says Tess. "A big salad should fill you up." 42

Greg's neck is stiff. "No problem!" says Tess. "A scarf should do the trick." 56

Kana has no pocket. "No problem!" says Tess. "This belt should fit you." 69

Deb can't paddle in the pond. "No problem!" says Tess. "Rent a raft." 82

Tess must step out. She has to rest. "No problem!" says Tess. "No problem at all." 98

Assessment 11

Lessons 67–72

Part 1

or al ea all

Part 2

instead forget wonderful

Part 3

Deb can't paddle in the pond.

Part 4

Step up! Step up! Tess has a stand!
Tess can help!

Tess helps all the animals. No problem is too big. No problem is too small.

T. Rex wants a snack. “No problem!” says Tess. “A big salad should fill you up.”

Greg’s neck is stiff. “No problem!” says Tess. “A scarf should do the trick.”

Kana has no pocket. “No problem!” says Tess. “This belt should fit you.”

Deb can’t paddle in the pond. “No problem!” says Tess. “Rent a raft.”

Tess must step out. She has to rest. “No problem!” says Tess. “No problem at all.”

Student ______________________ **Date** ______________

Assessment 12– Record Sheet

Lessons 73–80

Goals: 2 minutes for total assessment.
100% accuracy for Parts 1–3.
40 words correct per minute for Part 4.

Administration

(Administer to individual students. Check each box when the student achieves mastery.)

(Before administering the assessment, make a copy of this assessment form for each student being tested. Fill out the top of the forms with the students' names and testing date. Make a copy of student's Assessment 12.)

(Provide the student a copy of Assessment 12. Point to Part 1 on the student's page.)

We are going to find out how well you can say letter-sounds. When you touch under a letter-sound, say its sound. Get ready.
(Have students touch under the first letter-sound on their copy, and say, "Say the sound.")

j❒ k❒ s (is)❒ tch❒

Say the sound.
(Allow no more than 2 seconds for the student to respond. If student does not pronounce s as /z/ on the first try, remind him or her that s has another sound. If student responds correctly, check the box beside the letter-sound on your copy of the test. Repeat the procedure with the remaining sounds.)

(Point to Part 2 on the student's page.)
We are going to find out how well you can sound out words. You will say each part and then read the whole word the fast way. Get ready.

(Touch under the first word in Part 2 on the student's page.)

kitch en❒ mon ster❒ an i mals❒

Say each part, and then read the whole word.
(If the student responds correctly, check the box beside the word on your copy of the assessment. Repeat the procedure with the remaining words.)

(Point to Part 3 on the student's page.)
Now we will find out how well you read words in a sentence. *(Pause.)*

Read each sentence. If you know the word, say it. If you do not know the word, sound it out to yourself and say it fast.
(If the student responds correctly, check the box beside the sentence on your copy of the assessment. Fluency Goal: 2 seconds per word = 16 seconds.)

The ship is under the water! Abandon ship!❒

Student ____________________ Date ____________

Words Correct Per Minute ______

Fluency

1. Have student read the fluency passage.
2. Time student for one minute.
3. Determine and record the number of words student read correctly in one minute.
4. Fluency Goal = 40 words correct per minute

(Point to Part 4 on the student's page.)
I have a story I want you to read for me today. Read this story as fast as you can without making a mistake.

(Point to the first word of the story, and say, "Begin here." Start the stopwatch.)
As student reads, mark each error with a dark slash (/). At the end of one minute, place a double slash after the last word read in the passage (//).

Errors include:

- Omissions
- Insertions
- Mispronunciations not caused by a speech defect (for example, *house* instead of *home* or leaving off inflectional endings *-s, -ed,* and *-ing*)
- Words requiring more than 4 seconds

If a student cannot read a word within 4 seconds, tell student to go to the next word, put a slash (/) through the word on the record sheet, and point to the next word in the sentence.

After student reads the passage, praise his or her effort reading the passage. Do not offer praise for performance.

Determining number of words read correctly in one minute:

- Count the total number of words read.
- Subtract the number of errors (slashes).
- Write the words read correctly in one minute in the space provided.
- Fluency Goal = 40 words correct per minute

Remediation

(Before starting Lesson 81, review any letter-sounds or words students had trouble with on Assessment 12. Write on the marker board the items students missed. Using the model-lead-test strategy, review the letter-sounds and words with students.)

Ted had a hen in a pen. The hen was Henetta. Henetta's pen was a mess. 16

Ted said he would mend Henetta's pen. "I should mend it," Ted said. 29

"I am fed up!" Henetta sniffed. "Ted says he should mend my pen, but he still does
not mend it." 49

"I have had it!" Henetta said to the animals. Henetta ducked her head and flapped
out of the pen. 68

"Hen on the run!" called the animals as Henetta flapped past. "Hen on the run!"
called Ted. 85

Henetta flapped to the top of the pen. But she flapped too hard and fell into a bucket. 103

Assessment 12

Lessons 73–80

Part 1

j k s tch

Part 2

kitchen monster animals

Part 3

The ship is under the water!
Abandon ship!

Part 4

Ted had a hen in a pen. The hen was Henetta. Henetta's pen was a mess.

Ted said he would mend Henetta's pen. "I should mend it," Ted said.

"I am fed up!" Henetta sniffed. "Ted says he should mend my pen, but he still does not mend it."

"I have had it!" Henetta said to the animals. Henetta ducked her head and flapped out of the pen.

"Hen on the run!" called the animals as Henetta flapped past. "Hen on the run!" called Ted.

Henetta flapped to the top of the pen. But she flapped too hard and fell into a bucket.

Student ______________________________ **Date** ______________

Assessment 13– Record Sheet

Lessons 81–86

Goals: 2 minutes for total assessment. 100% accuracy for Parts 1–3. 43 words correct per minute for Part 4.

Administration

(Administer to individual students. Check each box when the student achieves mastery.)

(Before administering the assessment, make a copy of this assessment form for each student being tested. Fill out the top of the forms with the students' names and testing date. Make a copy of student's Assessment 13.)

(Provide the student a copy of Assessment 13. Point to Part 1 on the student's page.)

We are going to find out how well you can say letter-sounds. When you touch under a letter-sound, say its sound. Get ready.
(Have students touch under the first letter-sound on their copy, and say, "Say the sound.")

dge❐ ge❐ i (long)❐

a_e❐ gi❐

Say the sound.
(Allow no more than 2 seconds for the student to respond. Remind students that i has another sound if they provide only the short sound on the first try. If the student responds correctly, check the box beside the letter-sound on your copy of the test. Repeat the procedure with the remaining sounds.)

(Point to Part 2 on the student's page.)
We are going to find out how well you can read words. First you will read the underlined part. Then you will read the whole word. Get ready.
(Touch under the first word in Part 2 on the student's page.)

understand❐ judge❐ gentle❐

Read the underlined part, and then read the whole word.
(If the student responds correctly, check the box beside the word on your copy of the assessment. Repeat the procedure with the remaining words.)

(Point to Part 3 on the student's page.)
Now we will find out how well you read words in a sentence. *(Pause.)*

Read the sentence. If you know the word, say it. If you do not know the word, sound it out to yourself and say it fast.
(If the student responds correctly, check the box beside the sentence on your copy of the assessment. Fluency Goal: 2 seconds per word = 14 seconds.)

His shape made shade on the water.❐

Student ______________________________ **Date** ______________

Words Correct Per Minute ______

Fluency

1. Have student read the fluency passage.
2. Time student for one minute.
3. Determine and record the number of words student read correctly in one minute.
4. Fluency Goal = 43 words correct per minute

(Point to Part 4 on the student's page.)
I have a story I want you to read for me today. Read this story as fast as you can without making a mistake.

(Point to the first word of the story, and say, "Begin here." Start the stopwatch.)
As student reads, mark each error with a dark slash (/). At the end of one minute, place a double slash after the last word read in the passage (//).

Errors include:

- Omissions
- Insertions
- Mispronunciations not caused by a speech defect (for example, *house* instead of *home* or leaving off inflectional endings *-s, -ed,* and *-ing*)
- Words requiring more than 4 seconds

If a student cannot read a word within 4 seconds, tell student to go to the next word, put a slash (/) through the word on the record sheet, and point to the next word in the sentence.

After student reads the passage, praise his or her effort reading the passage. Do not offer praise for performance.

Determining number of words read correctly in one minute:

- Count the total number of words read.
- Subtract the number of errors (slashes).
- Write the words read correctly in one minute in the space provided.
- Fluency Goal = 43 words correct per minute

Remediation

(Before starting Lesson 87, review any letter-sounds or words students had trouble with on Assessment 13. Write on the marker board the items students missed. Using the model-lead-test strategy, review the letter-sounds and words with students.)

Gull and Crane were pals. 5

Gull and Crane did the same things. They waded in the same lake. They ate the same fish. 23

Gull and Crane fished together. Crane waded into the lake. His shape made shade on the water. 40

Fish swam into the shade. That was a mistake. 49

Snake had a nest across the lake. He was mad at Crane and Gull. They ate Snake's fish! 67

"I can get rid of them," hissed Snake. 75

Snake crossed the lake. He swam into the grass where Crane napped. 87

But Gull was awake. She called, "Snake in the lake! Snake in the lake! Watch the shade where you wade!" 107

"Hurray! They have left!" hissed Snake. But Snake still had no fish. 119

Assessment 13

Lessons 81–86

Part 1

dge ge i a_e gi

Part 2

understand judge gentle

Part 3

His shape made shade on the water.

Part 4

Gull and Crane were pals.

Gull and Crane did the same things. They waded in the same lake. They ate the same fish.

Gull and Crane fished together. Crane waded into the lake. His shape made shade on the water.

Fish swam into the shade. That was a mistake.

Snake had a nest across the lake. He was mad at Crane and Gull. They ate Snake's fish!

"I can get rid of them," hissed Snake.

Snake crossed the lake. He swam into the grass where Crane napped.

But Gull was awake. She called, "Snake in the lake! Snake in the lake! Watch the shade where you wade!"

"Hurray! They have left!" hissed Snake. But Snake still had no fish.

Student ______________________ Date ______________

Assessment 14– Record Sheet

Lessons 87–92

Goals: 2 minutes for total assessment. 100% accuracy for Parts 1–3. 46 words correct per minute for Part 4.

Administration

(Administer to individual students. Check each box when the student achieves mastery.)

(Before administering the assessment, make a copy of this assessment form for each student being tested. Fill out the top of the forms with the students' names and testing date. Make a copy of student's Assessment 14.)

(Provide the student a copy of Assessment 14. Point to Part 1 on the student's page.)

We are going to find out how well you can say letter-sounds. When you touch under a letter-sound, say its sound. Get ready.
(Have students touch under the first letter-sound on their copy, and say, "Say the sound.")

i_e❐ ee (need)❐ ci❐

ea (eagle)❐ _e❐ ce❐

Say the sound.
(Allow no more than 2 seconds for the student to respond. If the student responds correctly, check the box beside the letter-sound on your copy of the test. Repeat the procedure with the remaining sounds.)

(Point to Part 2 on the student's page.)
We are going to find out how well you can read words. First you will read the underlined part. Then you will read the whole word. Get ready.

(Touch under the first word in Part 2 on the student's page.)

gigantic❐ eagle❐ inside❐

Read the underlined part, and then read the whole word.
(If the student responds correctly, check the box beside the word on your copy of the assessment. Repeat the procedure with the remaining words.)

(Point to Part 3 on the student's page.)
Now we will find out how well you read words in a sentence. *(Pause.)*

Read the sentence. If you know the word, say it. If you do not know the word, sound it out to yourself and say it fast.
(If the student responds correctly, check the box beside the sentence on your copy of the assessment. Fluency Goal: 2 seconds per word = 24 seconds.)

The parade heads up a wide path and under a white bridge.❐

Student____ **Date**________________

Words Correct Per Minute _______

Fluency

1. Have student read the fluency passage.
2. Time student for one minute.
3. Determine and record the number of words student read correctly in one minute.
4. Fluency Goal = 46 words correct per minute

(Point to Part 4 on the student's page.)
I have a story I want you to read for me today. Read this story as fast as you can without making a mistake.

(Point to the first word of the story, and say, "Begin here." Start the stopwatch.)
As student reads, mark each error with a dark slash (/). At the end of one minute, place a double slash after the last word read in the passage (//).

Errors include:

- Omissions
- Insertions
- Mispronunciations not caused by a speech defect (for example, *house* instead of *home* or leaving off inflectional endings *-s, -ed,* and *-ing*)
- Words requiring more than 4 seconds

If a student cannot read a word within 4 seconds, tell student to go to the next word, put a slash (/) through the word on the record sheet, and point to the next word in the sentence.

After student reads the passage, praise his or her effort reading the passage. Do not offer praise for performance.

Determining number of words read correctly in one minute:

- Count the total number of words read.
- Subtract the number of errors (slashes).
- Write the words read correctly in one minute in the space provided.
- Fluency Goal = 46 words correct per minute

Remediation

(Before starting Lesson 93, review any letter-sounds or words students had trouble with on Assessment 14. Write on the marker board the items students missed. Using the model-lead-test strategy, review the letter-sounds and words with students.)

Tina rides a bike. Emma rides a trike. Kamara skates. 10

Nissa pulls April and her kite in the wagon. It is a parade! 23

Where is Spike? April finds him. "Jump in, Spike," she says. "It is time for the parade." 40

But Spike hates parades. He hides inside the shed. He barks and whines. "Do not mind him," says April. 59

The parade heads up a wide path and under a white bridge. "My kite!" yells April. "Where is my kite?" 79

Spike chases after the kite. He finds it and takes it back to the shed. 94

April smiles and pats Spike. "Spike saved my kite!" she says with pride. "He does not like parades. But he is a fine dog all the same." 121

Assessment 14

Lessons 87–92

Part 1

i_e ee ci

ea _e ce

Part 2

gigantic eagle inside

Part 3

The parade heads up a wide path and under a white bridge.

Part 4

Tina rides a bike. Emma rides a trike. Kamara skates.

Nissa pulls April and her kite in the wagon. It is a parade!

Where is Spike? April finds him. “Jump in, Spike,” she says. “It is time for the parade.”

But Spike hates parades. He hides inside the shed. He barks and whines. “Do not mind him,” says April.

The parade heads up a wide path and under a white bridge. “My kite!” yells April. “Where is my kite?”

Spike chases after the kite. He finds it and takes it back to the shed.

April smiles and pats Spike. “Spike saved my kite!” she says with pride. “He does not like parades. But he is a fine dog all the same.”

Student ______________________ **Date** ____________

Assessment 15– Record Sheet

Lessons 93–100

Goals: 2 minutes for total assessment.
100% accuracy for Parts 1–3.
50 words correct per minute for Part 4.

Administration

(Administer to individual students. Check each box when the student achieves mastery.)

(Before administering the assessment, make a copy of this assessment form for each student being tested. Fill out the top of the forms with the students' names and testing date. Make a copy of student's Assessment 15.)

(Provide the student a copy of Assessment 15. Point to Part 1 on the student's page.)

We are going to find out how well you can say letter-sounds. When you touch under a letter-sound, say its sound. Get ready.
(Have students touch under the first letter-sound on their copy, and say, "Say the sound.")

o_e☐ v☐ u_e☐

ol☐ _o☐

Sound it out.
(Allow no more than 2 seconds for the student to respond. If the student responds correctly, check the box beside the letter or group on your copy of the test. Repeat the procedure with the remaining sounds.)

(Point to Part 2 on the student's page.)
We are going to find out how well you can sound out words. You will say each part and then read the whole word the fast way. Get ready.

(Touch under the first word in Part 2 on the student's page.)

golden☐ refuse☐ haven't☐

Say each part, and then read the whole word.
(If the student responds correctly, check the box beside the word on your copy of the assessment. Repeat the procedure with the remaining words.)

(Point to Part 3 on the student's page.)
Now we will find out how well you read words in a sentence. *(Pause.)*

Read the sentence. If you know the word, say it. If you do not know the word, sound it out to yourself and say it fast.
(If the student responds correctly, check the box beside the sentence on your copy of the assessment. Fluency Goal: 2 seconds per word = 20 seconds.)

The branches are used to make baskets and fish traps.☐

Student____ **Date**________________

Words Correct Per Minute ________

Fluency

1. Have student read the fluency passage.
2. Time student for one minute.
3. Determine and record the number of words student read correctly in one minute.
4. Fluency Goal = 50 words correct per minute

(Point to Part 4 on the student's page.)
I have a story I want you to read for me today. Read this story as fast as you can without making a mistake.

(Point to the first word of the story, and say, "Begin here." Start the stopwatch.)
As student reads, mark each error with a dark slash (/). At the end of one minute, place a double slash after the last word read in the passage (//).

Errors include:

- Omissions
- Insertions
- Mispronunciations not caused by a speech defect (for example, *house* instead of *home* or leaving off inflectional endings *-s, -ed,* and *-ing*)
- Words requiring more than 4 seconds

If a student cannot read a word within 4 seconds, tell student to go to the next word, put a slash (/) through the word on the record sheet, and point to the next word in the sentence.

After student reads the passage, praise his or her effort reading the passage. Do not offer praise for performance.

Determining number of words read correctly in one minute:

- Count the total number of words read.
- Subtract the number of errors (slashes).
- Write the words read correctly in one minute in the space provided.
- Fluency Goal = 50 words correct per minute

Remediation

(Before starting Lesson 101, review any letter-sounds or words students had trouble with on Assessment 15. Write on the marker board the items students missed. Using the model-lead-test strategy, review the letter-sounds and words with students.)

Cupid is a mule. He lives in a forest close to the Amazon River. 14

Cupid does not like the forest. He does not like the bugs, the snakes, or the river animals. But Cupid does like music. 37

Alfonso is a trader. He cuts branches and trades them at the river. The branches are used to make baskets and traps. 59

After Alfonso cuts the branches, he makes a huge pile. Then he puts the pile on Cupid's back. 77

Cupid does not like the huge pile. He refuses to go to the river. Alfonso pushes and pulls, but Cupid does not budge. 100

At last Alfonso gets out his pipes. His pipes make fine music. The music amuses Cupid. 116

Cupid does not like the forest. He does not like the bugs, the snakes, or his huge pile. But Cupid does like music! 139

Assessment 15
Lessons 93–100

Part 1

o_e v u_e
ol _o

Part 2

golden refuse haven't

Part 3

The branches are used to make baskets and fish traps.

Part 4

Cupid is a mule. He lives in a forest close to the Amazon River.

Cupid does not like the forest. He does not like the bugs, the snakes, or the river animals. But Cupid does like music.

Alfonso is a trader. He cuts branches and trades them at the river. The branches are used to make baskets and traps.

After Alfonso cuts the branches, he makes a huge pile. Then he puts the pile on Cupid's back.

Cupid does not like the huge pile. He refuses to go to the river. Alfonso pushes and pulls, but Cupid does not budge.

At last Alfonso gets out his pipes. His pipes make fine music. The music amuses Cupid.

Cupid does not like the forest. He does not like the bugs, the snakes, or his huge pile. But Cupid does like music!

Student ______________________ Date ____________

Assessment 16–Record Sheet

Lessons 101–106

Goals: 2 minutes for total assessment. 100% accuracy for Parts 1–3. 53 words correct per minute for Part 4.

Administration

(Administer to individual students. Check each box when the student achieves mastery.)

(Before administering the assessment, make a copy of this assessment form for each student being tested. Fill out the top of the forms with the students' names and testing date. Make a copy of student's Assessment 16.)

(Provide the student a copy of Assessment 16. Point to Part 1 on the student's page.)

We are going to find out how well you can say letter-sounds. When you touch under a letter-sound, say its sound. Get ready.
(Have students touch under the first letter-sound on their copy, and say, "Say the sound.")

ay❐ y (long e)❐ qu❐

eer❐ ai❐ e_e❐

Say the sound.
(Allow no more than 2 seconds for the student to respond. If the student responds correctly, check the box beside the letter-sound on your copy of the test. Repeat the procedure with the remaining sounds.)

(Point to Part 2 on the student's page.)
We are going to find out how well you can read words. First you will read the underlined part. Then you will read the whole word. Get ready.

(Touch under the first word in Part 2 on the student's page.)

today❐ maintain❐ near❐

Read the underlined part, and then read the whole word.
(If the student responds correctly, check the box beside the word on your copy of the assessment. Repeat the procedure with the remaining words.)

(Point to Part 3 on the student's page.)
Now we will find out how well you read words in a sentence. *(Pause.)*

Read the sentence. If you know the word, say it. If you do not know the word, sound it out to yourself and say it fast.
(If the student responds correctly, check the box beside the sentence on your copy of the assessment. Fluency Goal: 2 seconds per word = 20 seconds.)

The queen squid and her pals had quite a feast.❐

Student____ Date________________

Words Correct Per Minute ______

Fluency

1. Have student read the fluency passage.
2. Time student for one minute.
3. Determine and record the number of words student read correctly in one minute.
4. Fluency Goal = 53 words correct per minute

(Point to Part 4 on the student's page.)
I have a story I want you to read for me today. Read this story as fast as you can without making a mistake.

(Point to the first word of the story, and say, "Begin here." Start the stopwatch.)
As student reads, mark each error with a dark slash (/). At the end of one minute, place a double slash after the last word read in the passage (//).

Errors include:

- Omissions
- Insertions
- Mispronunciations not caused by a speech defect (for example, *house* instead of *home* or leaving off inflectional endings *-s, -ed,* and *-ing*)
- Words requiring more than 4 seconds

If a student cannot read a word within 4 seconds, tell student to go to the next word, put a slash (/) through the word on the record sheet, and point to the next word in the sentence.

After student reads the passage, praise his or her effort reading the passage. Do not offer praise for performance.

Determining number of words read correctly in one minute:

- Count the total number of words read.
- Subtract the number of errors (slashes).
- Write the words read correctly in one minute in the space provided.
- Fluency Goal = 53 words correct per minute

Remediation

(Before starting Lesson 107, review any letter-sounds or words students had trouble with on Assessment 16. Write on the marker board the items students missed. Using the model-lead-test strategy, review the letter-sounds and words with students.)

A huge queen squid lived in the deep, dark sea. This kind queen squid had a squad of
sea pals to help her. 23

The huge queen squid squealed, "I need a meal!" 32

The queen's squad of sea pals heard her squeal. "It's time for the queen's meal," said
the pals. 50

The squad swam to get the queen her meal. A quiet shark swam near them. He needed
a meal too. 70

This time, the squad squealed! The queen heard the squeals. 80

The quick queen swam to her pals. She squirted black liquid into the shark's face.
The shark swam away. 99

The queen squid had saved her sea pals. The shark had no meal. The queen squid and
her pals had quite a feast! 122

Assessment 16

Lessons 101–106

Part 1

ay y qu

eer ai e_e

Part 2

today maintain near

Part 3

The queen squid and her
pals had quite a feast.

Part 4

A huge queen squid lived in the deep, dark sea. This kind queen squid had a squad of sea pals to help her.

The huge queen squid squealed, "I need a meal!"

The queen's squad of sea pals heard her squeal. "It's time for the queen's meal," said the pals.

The squad swam to get the queen her meal. A quiet shark swam near them. He needed a meal too.

This time, the squad squealed! The queen heard the squeals.

The quick queen swam to her pals. She squirted black liquid into the shark's face. The shark swam away.

The queen squid had saved her sea pals. The shark had no meal. The queen squid and her pals had quite a feast!

Student ______________________ **Date** ____________

Assessment 17—Record Sheet

Lessons 107–112

Goals: 2 minutes for total assessment. 100% accuracy for Parts 1–3. 56 words correct per minute for Part 4.

Administration

(Administer to individual students. Check each box when the student achieves mastery.)

(Before administering the assessment, make a copy of this assessment form for each student being tested. Fill out the top of the forms with the students' names and testing date. Make a copy of student's Assessment 17.)

(Provide the student a copy of Assessment 17. Point to Part 1 on the student's page.)

We are going to find out how well you can say letter-sounds. When you touch under a letter-sound, say its sound. Get ready.
(Have students touch under the first letter-sound on their copy, and say, "Say the sound.")

igh❒ are❒ eer❒ qu❒

Say the sound.
(Allow no more than 2 seconds for the student to respond. If the student responds correctly, check the box beside the letter-sound on your copy of the test. Repeat the procedure with the remaining sounds.)

(Point to Part 2 on the student's page.)
We are going to find out how well you can read words. First you will read the underlined part. Then you will read the whole word. Get ready.

(Touch under the first word in Part 2 on the student's page.)

carries❒ every❒ happier❒

Read the underlined part, and then read the whole word.
(If the student responds correctly, check the box beside the word on your copy of the assessment. Repeat the procedure with the remaining words.)

(Point to Part 3 on the student's page.)
Now we will find out how well you read words in a sentence. *(Pause.)*

Read the sentence. If you know the word, say it. If you do not know the word, sound it out to yourself and say it fast.
(If the student responds correctly, check the box beside the sentence on your copy of the assessment. Fluency Goal: 2 seconds per word = 12 seconds.)

A square has four equal sides.❒

Student ______________________________ Date ______________

Words Correct Per Minute ______

Fluency

1. Have student read the fluency passage.
2. Time student for one minute.
3. Determine and record the number of words student read correctly in one minute.
4. Fluency Goal = 56 words correct per minute

(Point to Part 4 on the student's page.) **I have a story I want you to read for me today. Read this story as fast as you can without making a mistake.**

(Point to the first word of the story, and say, "Begin here." Start the stopwatch.) As student reads, mark each error with a dark slash (/). At the end of one minute, place a double slash after the last word read in the passage (//).

Errors include:

- Omissions
- Insertions
- Mispronunciations not caused by a speech defect (for example, *house* instead of *home* or leaving off inflectional endings *-s, -ed,* and *-ing*)
- Words requiring more than 4 seconds

If a student cannot read a word within 4 seconds, tell student to go to the next word, put a slash (/) through the word on the record sheet, and point to the next word in the sentence.

After student reads the passage, praise his or her effort reading the passage. Do not offer praise for performance.

Determining number of words read correctly in one minute:

- Count the total number of words read.
- Subtract the number of errors (slashes).
- Write the words read correctly in one minute in the space provided.
- Fluency Goal = 56 words correct per minute

Remediation

(Before starting Lesson 113, review any letter-sounds or words students had trouble with on Assessment 17. Write on the marker board the items students missed. Using the model-lead-test strategy, review the letter-sounds and words with students.)

It is light. "Wake up! Wake up!" the birds call. 10

"The sun is high. The day is bright. Wake up!" 20

The opossum does not wake up. She sleeps in the daylight. Her babies hold on tight. 36

When it is night, she wakes up. She hunts for insects to feed her babies. 51

A dog frightens the opossum. The opossum freezes. She stays still and plays dead.
She "plays opossum." 68

Night is over. It begins to get light. The opossum returns to her tree. 82

"Go to sleep," she tells her babies. "We will play again tonight." 94

Assessment 17

Lessons 107–112

Part 1

igh are eer qu

Part 2

carries every happier

Part 3

A square has four equal sides.

Part 4

It is light. “Wake up! Wake up!” the birds call.

“The sun is high. The day is bright. Wake up!”

The opossum does not wake up. She sleeps in the daylight. Her babies hold on tight.

When it is night, she wakes up. She hunts for insects to feed her babies.

A dog frightens the opossum. The opossum freezes. She stays still and plays dead. She “plays opossum.”

Night is over. It begins to get light. The opossum returns to her tree.

“Go to sleep,” she tells her babies. “We will play again tonight.”

Student ______________________ **Date** ____________

Assessment 18–Record Sheet

Lessons 113–120

Goals: 2 minutes for total assessment. 100% accuracy for Parts 1–3. 60 words correct per minute for Part 4.

Administration

(Administer to individual students. Check each box when the student achieves mastery.)

(Before administering the assessment, make a copy of this assessment form for each student being tested. Fill out the top of the forms with the students' names and testing date. Make a copy of student's Assessment 18.)

(Provide the student a copy of Assessment 18. Point to Part 1 on the student's page.)

We are going to find out how well you can say letter-sounds. When I touch under a letter-sound, say its sound. Get ready. *(Have students touch under the first letter-sound on their copy.)*

ear☐ ol☐ ea☐ ci☐

igh☐ i_e☐ y (my)☐ ng☐

Sound it out.
(Allow no more than 2 seconds for the student to respond. If the student responds correctly, check the box beside the letter-sound on your copy of the test. Repeat the procedure with the remaining sound.)

(Point to Part 2 on the student's page.)
We are going to find out how well you can sound out words. You will say each part in your head and then read the whole word the fast way. Get ready.

(Touch under the first word in Part 2 on the student's page.)

de liv er ing☐ sprang☐

thank full y☐

Say each part in your head, and then read the whole word.
(If the student responds correctly, check the box beside the word on your copy of the assessment. Repeat the procedure with the remaining words.)

(Point to Part 3 on the student's page.)
Now we will find out how well you read words in a sentence. *(Pause.)*

Read the sentence. If you know the word, say it. If you do not know the word, sound it out to yourself and say it fast.
(If the student responds correctly, check the box beside the sentence on your copy of the assessment. Fluency Goal: 1 second per word = 14 seconds.)

Tell Queen Fay that King Ray may add the right spice at dinner tonight.☐

Student____ **Date**________________

Words Correct Per Minute _______

Fluency

1. Have student read the fluency passage.
2. Time student for one minute.
3. Determine and record the number of words student read correctly in one minute.
4. Fluency Goal = 60 words correct per minute

(Point to Part 4 on the student's page.)
I have a story I want you to read for me today. Read this story as fast as you can without making a mistake.

(Point to the first word of the story, and say, "Begin here." Start the stopwatch.)
As student reads, mark each error with a dark slash (/). At the end of one minute, place a double slash after the last word read in the passage (//).

Errors include:

- Omissions
- Insertions
- Mispronunciations not caused by a speech defect (for example, *house* instead of *home* or leaving off inflectional endings *-s, -ed,* and *-ing*)
- Words requiring more than 4 seconds

If a student cannot read a word within 4 seconds, tell student to go to the next word, put a slash (/) through the word on the record sheet, and point to the next word in the sentence.

After student reads the passage, praise his or her effort reading the passage. Do not offer praise for performance.

Determining number of words read correctly in one minute:

- Count the total number of words read.
- Subtract the number of errors (slashes).
- Write the words read correctly in one minute in the space provided.
- Fluency Goal = 60 words correct per minute

Remediation

(Before completing Level 1, review any letter-sounds or words students had trouble with on Assessment 18. Write on the marker board the items students missed. Using the model-lead-test strategy, review the letter-sounds and words with students.)

King Ray was late. "My wife will be mad if I make her wait," he said. "I must tell her that I will be late." 25

So King Ray told his page: "Please tell Queen Fay that I may not be on time for dinner tonight." 45

His page told a squire: "Tell Queen Fay that King Ray may put on a bright leaf for dinner tonight." 65

The squire told Lord Jay: "Tell Queen Fay that King Ray may sail a fancy kite before dinner tonight." 84

Lord Jay told a mayor: "Tell Queen Fay that King Ray may have berries on ice for dinner tonight." 103

The mayor told a duchess: "Tell Queen Fay that King Ray may need some nice rice for dinner tonight." 122

Assessment 18

Lessons 113–120

Part 1

ear ol ea ci

igh i_e y ng

Part 2

delivering sprang thankfully

Part 3

Tell Queen Fay that King Ray
may add the right spice
at dinner tonight.

Part 4

King Ray was late. "My wife will be mad if I make her wait," he said. "I must tell her that I will be late."

So King Ray told his page: "Please tell Queen Fay that I may not be on time for dinner tonight."

His page told a squire: "Tell Queen Fay that King Ray may put on a bright leaf for dinner tonight."

The squire told Lord Jay: "Tell Queen Fay that King Ray may sail a fancy kite before dinner tonight."

Lord Jay told a mayor: "Tell Queen Fay that King Ray may have berries on ice for dinner tonight."

The mayor told a duchess: "Tell Queen Fay that King Ray may need some nice rice for dinner tonight."

Make one set for each student.

sh	th	ch
o	u	
a	e	i

Reading Certificate

Week Ending ______________________

I know the sounds of these letters ______________________

My new tricky words are ______________________

I can spell ______________________

I can stretch ______________________

I read these stories this week. Please listen to me read the stories, and then sign the front of the books and send them back to school.

Teacher's Comments:

Reading Certificate

Week Ending ______________________

I know the sounds of these letters ______________________

My new tricky words are ______________________

I can spell ______________________

I can stretch ______________________

I read these stories this week. Please listen to me read the stories, and then sign the front of the books and send them back to school.

Teacher's Comments:

Hora de Brillar

Boletín Familiar

Certificado de Leer

Semana que termina____________________

Conozco los sonidos de estas letras____________________

Mis nuevas palabras difíciles son____________________

Puedo deletrear____________________

Puedo estirar____________________

He leído estos cuentos esta semana. Por favor escúcheme leer los cuentos y firme en el frente de los libros para devolver a la escuela.

Comentario de la profesora:

Certificado de Leer

Semana que termina____________________

Conozco los sonidos de estas letras____________________

Mis nuevas palabras difíciles son____________________

Puedo deletrear____________________

Puedo estirar____________________

He leído estos cuentos esta semana. Por favor escúcheme leer los cuentos y firme en el frente de los libros para devolver a la escuela.

Comentario de la profesora: